Student Workbook

by
Bonnie L. Walker

AGS Publishing
Circle Pines, Minnesota 55014-1796
1-800-328-2560

Printed in the United States of America

ISBN 0-7854-2927-1
Product Number 93473

A 0 9 8 7 6 5 4

Table of Contents

Identifying Sentences

Directions Read each group of words. Underline the groups of words that are sentences. Circle the groups of words that are sentence fragments. Then add word to each sentence fragment to make it a complete sentence. Write the sentence on the line.

EXAMPLE
A duck made a nest in the bushes next to the house.
(native to Australia)   The wallaby is native to Australia.

1. The Audubon Zoo in New Orleans.

2. Provides a home for 1,800 animals.

3. None of the animals lives in cages.

4. White alligators with blue eyes live in a swamp.

5. The world's only urban swamp.

6. Blue whales are the biggest whales in the world.

7. A flock of birds flying.

8. To answer a letter.

9. The ancient Romans built many good roads.

10. An elephant's skin is thick and wrinkled.

Capitalization and End Punctuation

Directions Read each group of words. Find the sentences and write them in order on a separate sheet of paper. Capitalize the first word in each sentence. Put a punctuation mark at the end.

EXAMPLE everyone in my family likes yogurt our favorite flavor is strawberry we often have yogurt for a snack.

Everyone in my family likes yogurt.
We often have yogurt for a snack.
Our favorite flavor is strawberry.

---

1. in the spring we planted a garden we planted green peppers and squash first later we planted tomatoes

2. my grandmother sent me a CD for my birthday I wrote a letter to thank her she was pleased

3. my friends and I started a singing group we practice five times a month I think we need more practice

4. today it rained the streets were flooded we could not get our car out of the garage

5. there was an announcement in the newspaper about an upcoming concert tickets go on sale next week I would love to go to that concert

6. yesterday my sister went to the bank she wanted to deposit her paycheck she also wanted to get some quarters for the machines at the laundry

7. I saw an announcement on the bulletin board the coach is having tryouts for the soccer team should my friend and I go

8. every year the garden club has a sale the club members offer many different kinds of plants they tell customers all about the plants

9. what two things must a writer do first a writer must think of an idea to write about he or she also must decide how to write about the idea

10. my new digital camera takes amazing pictures I love photography I would like to take a class to learn more about it

Using End Punctuation

Directions Add the correct end punctuation mark to each sentence.

 EXAMPLE What is your favorite book
What is your favorite book?

1. Have you ever read *The Red Pony*

2. It is a story by John Steinbeck

3. What a wonderful story it is

4. *The Red Pony* was written in 1933

5. Would you like to read it for your next book report

6. His father told Jody to feed and clean the horse every day

7. Remember his name

8. Jody's father was very stern

9. He gave Jody a red pony to care for

10. "Feed him and clean him every day"

11. The pony's name was Gabilan

12. At first Gabilan was scared and wild

13. The pony and Jody became friends

14. Jody loved that pony so much

15. Do you want to know what happened next

16. Read the book and find the answer

17. *The Red Pony* is still a popular book

18. Maybe it is popular because it is so short

19. *The Red Pony* is a heartwarming story

20. Have you ever seen the movie

Identifying the Purpose of a Sentence

Directions Write the purpose of each sentence on the line. Choose from
the following:

Statement   **Question**   **Command**   **Exclamation**

Add correct punctuation at the end of each sentence.

(**EXAMPLE**)   The ship leaves at noon.   ___Statement___

1. Having a bank account is important   _____

2. What kind of bank account do you have   _____

3. Can you have more than one type of account   _____

4. Yes, you can   _____

5. I have enough money to buy a stereo   _____

6. Eliza explained that she has just opened her account   _____

7. I am saving to buy a car when I graduate   _____

8. Please tell me when I have enough   _____

9. How much is enough   _____

10. You should know soon   _____

11. I have plenty of time to decide   _____

12. Mrs. Choy has two accounts   _____

13. Does she have a checking account   _____

14. Please explain how to open a checking account   _____

15. What is the purpose of a checking account   _____

16. Can you use a checking account in place of cash   _____

17. It is safer than cash   _____

18. Derek, write me a check   _____

19. How do you choose the correct bank   _____

20. Do research before choosing a bank   _____

Creating Dialogue

Directions   Rewrite each sentence on the line. Add quotation marks, commas, and end punctuation marks where they are needed.

EXAMPLE   Robby asked Where are we going
            Robby asked, "Where are we going?"

1. Let's go camping next weekend Brandon suggested

2. That sounds good to me Derek agreed

3. I have a tent. Do you have any equipment Brandon asked

4. Well said Derek I have a sleeping bag

5. What about a stove asked Brandon

6. Derek said I think that I can borrow one from my boss

7. We will hike about 10 miles before we make camp Brandon said

8. Derek added Then we'll catch fish for our dinner

9. We will crawl inside our sleeping bags said Brandon. We'll be warm inside the tent

10. Do you think we'll see any bears this year asked Derek

11. No chance said Brandon. We almost never see a bear up there

12. Anyway, they are always friendly said Derek

13. I just remembered something Brandon said

14. I think I have a baseball game this weekend he exclaimed

15. Too bad said Derek. That would have been fun, too

Writing Direct and Indirect Quotations

Directions Change the indirect quotations (1–5) to direct quotations.
Change the direct quotations (6–10) to indirect quotations.
Write the new sentences on the lines. Use correct punctuation.

EXAMPLE   Jan said that she liked a cup of hot tea in the morning.
  "I like a cup of hot tea in the morning," said Jan.

1. Amber asked Derek if he wanted a second piece of cake.

_____

2. Derek reminded her that he was watching his weight.

_____

3. Amber laughed and said he should have told her sooner.

_____

4. She said she could have given him an apple for dessert.

_____

5. Derek said that he would rather have cake.

_____

6. "Sit down and have breakfast," Brandon's father said.

_____

7. "Breakfast is the most important meal of the day," he continued.

_____

8. Brandon shrugged, "But I'm in a hurry, Dad."

_____

9. "Besides," Brandon said, "I'm not hungry in the morning."

_____

10. "I won't take no for an answer, son," Brandon's father said firmly.

_____

Writing Sentences to Answer Questions

Directions Answer each question with a sentence. Use correct
capitalization and end punctuation.

EXAMPLE   What is your favorite holiday?
            My favorite holiday is Thanksgiving.

1. What is today's date?

_____

2. What is your name?

_____

3. How old are you?

_____

4. In which state do you live?

_____

5. What is the capital of your state?

_____

6. Who is the president of the United States?

_____

7. What is your favorite color?

_____

8. What is your teacher's name?

_____

9. What is your favorite sport or hobby?

_____

10. What is the name of the last movie you saw?

_____

Making Subjects and Verbs Agree

Directions The subject of each sentence is in bold. The verbs are in parentheses. Complete each sentence by writing the correct form of the verb on the line.

EXAMPLE   One **girl** _____walks_____ home. (walk, walks)

1. **Both** of my friends _____ going to the party. (is, are)

2. **Eliza** _____ a party every year. (gives, give)

3. **She** _____ the best snacks you ever tasted. (makes, make)

4. **Eliza** _____ a recreation room in her basement. (has, have)

5. **Her mother and father** _____ upstairs. (stays, stay)

6. **Eliza** usually _____ Jason as her date. (invites, invite)

7. **He and Eliza** _____ parties. (loves, love)

8. **They** both _____ pizza. (likes, like)

9. **Brandon** always _____ there early. (gets, get)

10. **Everyone** _____ that they'd better come on time. (knows, know)

11. Eliza's **father** always _____ the same thing. (does, do)

12. There _____ a large **clock** on the wall. (is, are)

13. Her **dad** _____ downstairs around midnight. (comes, come)

14. **He** _____ the clock. (checks, check)

15. **Everybody** _____ home. (goes, go)

Subjects and Verbs

Directions The subject of each sentence is bold. Choose the verb in parentheses that correctly completes the sentence. Write the verb on the line.

EXAMPLE   **Derek** ____is____ excited about getting a computer for a graduation present. (is, are)

1. **He** _____ to receive many gifts. (hopes, hope)

2. Both **Amber and Eliza** _____ parties. (enjoys, enjoy)

3. **Everyone** _____ about the graduation party. (knows, know)

4. **Each** of the girls _____ excellent cookies. (makes, make)

5. **Amber** usually _____ in the front of the class. (sits, sit)

6. **One** of the soccer players _____ football, too. (likes, like)

7. The **dog** _____ over the gate all the time. (jumps, jump)

8. Some **students** _____ all their homework correctly. (completes, complete)

9. Several **girls** _____ Eliza every night. (calls, call)

10. Neither **Amber** nor **Eliza** _____ to watch TV. (wants, want)

11. Many **people** _____ to watch the parade. (stays, stay)

12. A **few** of them _____ along with the music. (claps, clap)

13. There _____ several **routes** through the park. (is, are)

14. Either **Derek** or **Brandon** _____ to drive. (plans, plan)

15. **Everybody** _____ food and hiking boots. (brings, bring)

Replacing Nouns with Pronouns

Directions Change each noun in bold to a pronoun. Write the pronoun on the line. Remember, a pronoun must agree in number and gender with the word it replaces.

(**EXAMPLE**)   Where did **Mary** go?   _____she_____
                Nancy and Joanie are sisters.   _____They_____

---

1. **Derek and Eliza** agreed to meet for lunch.

_____

2. Derek planned to meet Eliza after **Eliza's** French class.

_____

3. **Eliza's** French teacher is Mrs. Bernstein.

_____

4. Mrs. Bernstein had given **Mrs. Bernstein's** class a long assignment.

_____

5. Eliza did not understand **the assignment** completely.

_____

6. **Eliza** was still talking to Mrs. Bernstein about it when Derek arrived.

_____

7. Derek paced back and forth because Eliza was making **Eliza and Derek** late for lunch.

_____

8. Finally, **Eliza** came out of the classroom.

_____

9. "I'm sorry to keep you waiting," Eliza said to **Derek.**

_____

10. "OK, but let's hurry. The special today is pizza, and I don't want to miss **pizza**," said Derek.

_____

Words That Are Capitalized

Directions Write a proper noun for each common noun.

(**EXAMPLE**)   author   <u>Agatha Christie</u>

---

1. state   _____

2. city   _____

3. movie   _____

4. book   _____

5. song   _____

6. continent   _____

7. ocean   _____

8. friend   _____

9. school   _____

10. river   _____

11. restaurant   _____

12. food store   _____

13. airline   _____

14. month   _____

15. holiday   _____

Directions Write a common noun for each proper noun.

(**EXAMPLE**)   Labor Day   <u>holiday</u>

---

16. Algebra II   _____

17. Chinese   _____

18. December   _____

19. Memorial Day   _____

20. *Beauty and the Beast*   _____

21. Indian Ocean   _____

22. San Francisco   _____

23. Canada   _____

24. Andrew Jackson   _____

25. South America   _____

26. Lake Erie   _____

27. *Great Expectations*   _____

28. Saturday   _____

29. William Shakespeare   _____

30. Colorado   _____

Identifying Verbs and Verb Phrases

Directions Write the verb or verb phrase in each sentence on the line.
Circle each helping verb.

EXAMPLE I should help my mom with dinner. _____(should) help_____

1. She will be late because of the traffic.

   _____

2. Derek has visited my family for many years.

   _____

3. The teacher will collect the homework assignment now.

   _____

4. He jogged five miles in gym class.

   _____

5. Eliza is watching the videos with Derek.

   _____

6. They stopped at the store.

   _____

7. I should receive my yearbook today.

   _____

8. Amber purchased a beautiful dress.

   _____

9. Derek is taking pictures with his camera.

   _____

10. The editor of the yearbook has asked for pictures of the track team.

    _____

Using Regular and Irregular Verbs

Directions On the line, write the form of the verb in parentheses that correctly completes the sentence.

EXAMPLE Amber has ____thought____ about taking Lucky to obedience classes. (think)

1. Lucky has _____ Amber a ball. (bring)

2. Amber's dog has _____ the ball in the air. (catch)

3. At the obedience class, Amber _____ her dog around the ring. (lead)

4. Last year, one of the dogs _____ a blue ribbon at a dog show. (win)

5. The instructor has _____ this class for many years. (teach)

6. She has _____ about a dog show coming up next week. (hear)

7. After each trick, she _____ her dog a treat. (feed)

8. Amber _____ a bag of treats for Lucky at the store. (buy)

9. She has _____ Lucky to three classes so far. (take)

10. After two classes, Lucky _____ to show improvement. (begin)

11. By the third class, Lucky had _____ everything he had learned. (forget)

12. Amber _____ Lucky a treat. (give)

13. Lucky quickly _____ down. (sit)

14. "I _____ you could do it!" Amber smiled. (know)

15. When it was time for the next class, Amber could not find Lucky. He had _____ under the bed. (hide)

More Irregular Verbs

Directions Circle the verb error in each sentence. Rewrite the sentence correctly on the line.

EXAMPLE   A bag of popcorn (costed) three dollars.
           A bag of popcorn cost three dollars.

---

1. Last week at baseball practice Brandon fell and splitted his lip.

_____

2. Derek has readed that yoga is good exercise.

_____

3. "Yesterday I done my homework early," said Brandon.

_____

4. "Have you did your grammar homework?" asked Derek.

_____

5. "Where has my tennis racket went?"

_____

6. Is it losted again?

_____

7. I think that Brandon has went home.

_____

8. The water bottle bursted when it hit the tennis court.

_____

9. "I done as much practicing as I needed to," said Derek.

_____

10. Where have you setted the new can of tennis balls?

_____

Basic English Composition

Possessives and Plurals

Directions Decide whether each noun in bold is singular or plural. Write *S* for singular or *P* for plural on the line by each noun.

EXAMPLE
The **members** listen to **evidence**.
members _____P_____
evidence _____S_____

---

1. One day **Mrs. Choy** got a letter in the **mail**.

   Mrs. Choy _____   mail _____

2. The **letter** said that she had jury **duty**.

   letter _____   duty _____

3. A **jury** is made up of 12 **people**.

   jury _____   people _____

4. A jury judges a defendant's **guilt** or **innocence**.

   guilt _____   innocence _____

5. All 12 **men** and **women** must agree.

   men _____   women _____

Directions The apostrophes have been left out of these phrases. Read each phrase and write it on the line. Put an apostrophe in the correct place.

EXAMPLE
the ladys purse _____the lady's purse_____
the mens club _____the men's club_____

---

6. the wolfs howl   _____

7. the calves pen   _____

8. Ambers dog Lucky   _____

9. the childrens room _____

10. the Smiths vacation _____

Choosing Between Words That Sound Alike

Directions Choose the word in parentheses that correctly completes the
sentence. Write the word on the line.

EXAMPLE Please _____write_____ your answer on this page. (right, write)

---

1. When are you planning to _____ your aunt a letter? (right, write)

2. What is the _____ answer to the question? (right, write)

3. Many people _____ with their _____ hand. (right, write)

4. Derek looked left and _____ before he crossed the road. (right, write)

5. Brandon forgot to _____ his name on his test paper. (right, write)

6. Are you going to _____ the _____ first? (pear, pair, pare)

7. The _____ become ripe in August every year. (pears, pairs, pares)

8. Amber and Eliza are quite a _____ . (pear, pair, pare)

9. Please _____ these potatoes for dinner. (pear, pair, pare)

10. Derek needed a new _____ of track shoes. (pear, pair, pare)

11. Is there a golf _____ near your home? (course, coarse)

12. Sometimes wool can be very _____ . (course, coarse)

13. We followed the _____ of the river to its mouth. (course, coarse)

14. The pepper had been ground to be very _____ . (course, coarse)

15. Mrs. Gonzalez signed up for a swimming _____ . (course, coarse)

Choosing the Correct Word

Directions Choose the word that correctly completes each sentence. On the line, write *desert* or *dessert*.

EXAMPLES A tall cactus grew in the ____desert____.
The mice decided to ____desert____ the barn.
Tim's favorite ____dessert____ is ice cream.

1. What would you like tonight for _____ ?

2. I would not want to be lost in the Sahara. It is a huge _____ !

3. There is a _____ in Arizona. Have you been there?

4. I hope you will not _____ me if I need help.

5. Fresh fruit makes a good _____ .

6. A captain must never _____ his or her ship.

7. After the main course, people sometimes have _____ .

8. The faithful dog would not _____ its master.

9. Eliza's favorite _____ is chocolate pudding.

10. If you travel across a _____ , take plenty of water!

Directions Write five sentences using *desert* or *dessert*.

11. _____

12. _____

13. _____

14. _____

15. _____

Identifying Contractions and Possessive Pronouns

Directions Choose the correct word from each pair in parentheses and write it on the line.

(**EXAMPLE**)   _____Whose_____ tennis shoes are these? (Who's, Whose)

---

1. Hurry up! _____ almost time to go. (It's, Its)

2. Is _____ race first or second? (you're, your)

3. If _____ late, you will miss the race. (you're, your)

4. "_____ ride is waiting for you!" (You're, Your)

5. I can't believe it! I think _____ starting to rain. (it's, its)

6. _____ a 90 percent chance it will stop soon. (There's, Theirs)

7. Do you see that huge thundercloud over _____ ? (there, their)

8. Where _____ a will, _____ a way. (there's, theirs)

9. _____ that guy over there? (Who's, Whose)

10. _____ team is expected to win? (Who's, Whose)

Directions Write the words in bold as contractions. Write the contractions on the lines.

(**EXAMPLE**)   Amber **had not** been to a track meet before.   _____hadn't_____

---

11. Sit down. I **cannot** see the race.   _____

12. It **is not** time for the race to start.   _____

13. I **do not** think so.   _____

14. You **should not** be on the track, Derek.   _____

15. **I am** going right now.   _____

Making Singular Nouns Plural

Directions Rewrite the nouns in parentheses by changing each one to its plural form. Write the plural form on the line.

EXAMPLE By 1900 more people lived in (city) than on farms.   _____cities_____

1. The (leaf) fell from the trees. _____

2. They sat on the (bench) in the park. _____

3. Cats are said to have nine (life). _____

4. Every year we have to pay more (tax). _____

5. The (baby) played with the toys. _____

6. All the (shoe) in the store were on sale. _____

7. The (monkey) chattered loudly. _____

8. I found several (penny) in my pocket. _____

9. The (sheep) ambled up the hill. _____

10. The (child) played party games. _____

11. The (goose) eat the grass by the pond. _____

12. The (building) were torn down. _____

13. I love fresh red (tomato). _____

14. Put the (knife) on the right. _____

15. Mr. Choy found his (key). _____

Writing Plural Nouns

Directions Write a sentence that uses the plural form of each word.

_____

(EXAMPLES) Herz _____ The Herzes had a party last week. _____
1950 _____ The space race began in the 1950s. _____

_____

1. Chevez

_____

2. 1800

_____

3. Choy

_____

4. Karas

_____

5. *e*

_____

Directions On the line, write the plural form of the word in bold.

_____

(EXAMPLE) My cousin got **B** in most of his English courses. _____ Bs _____

_____

6. Seven grandchildren were born in the **1990**. _____

7. The **Heinz** came from Germany. _____

8. The **Lopez** arrived at the party. _____

9. The band played music from the **1980**. _____

10. The photographer took a picture of the **Bendix**. _____

Spelling Words with *ie* or *ei*

Directions Look at each pair of words. Circle the word that is spelled correctly. Use this rule:

Put *i* before *e*
Except after *c*
Or when sounded like *a*
As in *neighbor* and *weigh*.

EXAMPLE   cheif   (chief)

1.	receive	recieve	**6.**	piece	peice
2.	neice	niece	**7.**	sleigh	sliegh
3.	freind	friend	**8.**	theif	thief
4.	shreik	shriek	**9.**	acheive	achieve
5.	feild	field	**10.**	ceiling	cieling

There are some exceptions to the rule above. When the *ei* combination has a "long" vowel sound, it is usually spelled *ei*. For example, *either* (ei = "ee") and *height* (ei = "eye").

11.	protein	protien	**14.**	niether	neither
12.	sieze	seize	**15.**	achievement	acheivement
13.	leisure	liesure	**16.**	yeild	yield

Some words do not follow the exception rule either. For example, *ancient*.

17.	weird	wierd	**19.**	foriegn	foreign
18.	sceince	science	**20.**	cashier	casheir

Adding Endings to Words

Directions Read each sentence. Look at the word and ending in parentheses. Write the word with its ending on the line. You might need to double the final consonant.

EXAMPLE Derek was a _____winner_____ at the track meet. (win + er)

1. Derek Anderson is a _____ . (run + er)

2. He enjoys _____ track. (run + ing)

3. Sarah is _____ hurdles today. (jump + ing)

4. "I am glad the track is not _____ ," said Derek. (mud + y)

5. This spring has been the _____ ever. (wet + est)

6. When the race _____ , the team went out for dinner. (end + ed)

7. "We _____ the day!" said Derek. (control + ed)

8. This is only the _____ of the season. (begin + ing)

9. Have you _____ anything? (forgot + en)

10. What a _____ lots of practice makes! (differ + ence)

11. I hope it does not get any _____ . (hot + er)

12. This may be the _____ day of the year so far. (hot + est)

13. We are fortunate to have good _____ . (equip + ment)

14. Am I _____ anything? (forget + ing)

15. What a terrific day for _____ a new record! (set + ing)

Knowing When to Drop the Final *e*

Directions Put each word and ending together and write the new word on the line. Remember to keep the silent final *e* when the ending begins with a consonant. Drop the silent final *e* when the ending begins with a vowel.

EXAMPLES   taste + ful   _____tasteful_____
                          taste + y   _____tasty_____

1. hope + ful   _____
2. use + less   _____
3. care + ing   _____
4. change + ing   _____
5. agree + ment   _____

6. adore + able   _____
7. arrange + ment   _____
8. wonder + ful   _____
9. care + ful   _____
10. freeze + ing   _____

Directions Look for the misspelled words in these sentences. Cross out each misspelled word and write it correctly on the line.

EXAMPLE   Derek and Brandon are ~~practiceing~~ their tennis serves at the park.   _____practicing_____

11. Derek is hopeful his serveing will improve.   _____

12. "That is debateable," said Brandon.   _____

13. We have a tickleish situation ahead of us.   _____

14. There is a lot of excitment about the next tennis match.   _____

15. Derek and Brandon find it usful to practice every day.   _____

16. If we get carless, we are sure to lose.   _____

17. "Our opponents had scarey serves," said Brandon.   _____

18. "Their backhands were particularly troublsome," said Derek.   _____

19. Brandon is hopeing they will play better next time.   _____

20. We can achieve victory if we work together instead of separatly.   _____

Correcting Spelling Demons

Directions Find and circle the spelling errors in the story. Write the words correctly on the line below each sentence.

EXAMPLE   It wouldn't be (plesant) to camp out in (Febuary)!

_____ pleasant, February _____

1. Derek and Brandon are leaveing on a camping trip next Wensday.

_____

2. They are excited because the whether is suposed to be good.

_____

3. They have goten all of their supplies togather.

_____

4. Derek bought close and fillm at the store.

_____

5. Brandon bought some boots a freind reccommended.

_____

6. The boys' parunts will drive them to the camp were they are staying.

_____

7. Brandon said, "The discription makes the camp sound very intresting."

_____

8. The too boys were awake early the next morening.

_____

9. Finaly everything was in the car, which was suprising.

_____

10. Brandon's dad asked, "Are all these things neccessary for you're trip?"

_____

11. Both boys replyed, "Were ready for anything!"

_____

12. They had a wonerful experience.

_____

13. They hiked threw the mountains and swam acros a lake.

_____

14. "Did you sea any wild animuls?" asked Derek's mom.

_____

15. "Onse we saw some unusal deer," said Derek.

_____

Fixing Run-On Sentences

Directions Read each group of words. Three sentences have been run together. Find the beginning and the end of each complete thought. Write the three sentences on the lines. Capitalize and punctuate each sentence correctly.

EXAMPLE
Derek loves baseball he plays every Saturday he goes to a lot of games
Derek loves baseball.
He plays every Saturday.
He goes to a lot of games.

---

1. The baseball game begins at 7:30 P.M. pick me up at 6:30 I don't want to be late

_____

_____

_____

2. The Wolves are playing the Cougars the Wolves have won six games the Cougars have won four

_____

_____

_____

3. The batter hit the ball hard the left fielder ran back the ball went over the fence

_____

_____

_____

4. it was a home run the crowd cheered wildly people love to see home runs

_____

_____

_____

5. the batter jogged around the bases he waved to the crowd his teammates met him at home plate

_____

_____

_____

Identifying Sentence Fragments

Directions Label each group of words as a *sentence* or a *fragment*.
Then add words to each fragment to make it a sentence.
Write the sentence on the line.

(EXAMPLE)   When he was here.   ____fragment____
                ____When he was here, we saw each other every day.____

---

1. I am sorry for not calling you back.   _____

_____

2. The store around the corner.   _____

_____

3. Wrote a letter yesterday.   _____

_____

4. Derek completed his homework assignment.   _____

_____

5. Answered the phone.   _____

_____

6. From my sisters and brothers.   _____

_____

7. I cannot wait to go to the beach next week.   _____

_____

8. On the computer all day.   _____

_____

9. Went to work at eight o'clock.   _____

_____

10. The book I read was quite long and detailed.   _____

_____

Adding Adjectives and Adverbs

Directions Read the sentences. Write an adjective or an adverb on each
line to complete each sentence.

EXAMPLE The _____ boy works _____ on his homework assignment.
The __little__ boy works __carefully__ on his homework assignment.

1. I like _____ ice cream with _____ and _____ sauce on it.

2. Derek drives _____ in _____ weather.

3. The _____ girl asked Derek to go to the _____ movie on
_____ night.

4. The _____ runner was _____ and _____ after a(n)
_____ run.

5. The _____ exam lasted _____ hours and was _____ difficult.

6. In _____ class we had to run _____ miles around the
_____ track.

7. The _____ library has _____ books we can use for
_____ projects.

8. The _____ and _____ dinner was _____ lasagna.

9. The florist made a(n) _____ arrangement for the _____ wedding.

10. We _____ go to the _____ beach on the _____ weekend.

Using Adjectives and Adverbs to Compare

Directions Choose the correct form of the word in parentheses.
Write your answer on the line.

EXAMPLE   Laura is ____younger____ than Shirley is. (younger, youngest)

---

1. Of the two pizzas, which do you like _____? (better, best)

2. Out of all the members of the track team, Derek can run the _____ . (faster, fastest)

3. Chocolate fudge is _____ than an apple. (more satisfying, most satisfying)

4. Which is the _____ expensive out of those three dresses? (less, least)

5. The book was _____ than the movie. (worse, worst)

6. She is _____ than her little sister. (smaller, smallest)

7. Derek is the _____ person in the group. (older, oldest)

8. I drive _____ than my dad. (slower, slowest)

9. In my family, Brandon cooks the _____ dinners. (better, best)

10. Eliza received her report card and was _____ than I. (happier, happiest)

Directions Write five sentences with adjectives or adverbs. Use each
adjective or adverb in one of its three forms: positive,
comparative, superlative. Identify the form you used by
writing it on the line following the sentence.

11. _____

    _____

12. _____

    _____

13. _____

    _____

14. _____

    _____

15. _____

    _____

Identifying Prepositional Phrases

Directions Find the prepositional phrase or phrases in each sentence.
Write each phrase on the line.

EXAMPLE   I received a letter from my friend.   <u>from my friend</u>

1. She found the cat under the table.   _____

2. Eliza asked if she could go with us.   _____

3. Derek is at the movies.   _____

4. The guest speaker will arrive by plane.   _____

5. For lunch we will order pizza.   _____

6. Derek sits in the front of the class.   _____

_____

7. The phone rang continually from noon until one o'clock.   _____

_____

8. Amber picked me up at the bank.   _____

9. I like ice cream with fresh strawberries.   _____

10. They go to the library almost every night.   _____

Using Conjunctions to Connect and Combine

Directions Combine each group of short sentences into one longer sentence. Use conjunctions. Make sure that the verb tense agrees with the subject.

EXAMPLE   Amber bowls on Saturdays.   Brandon bowls on Saturdays.   Eliza bowls on Saturdays.
<u>Amber, Brandon, and Eliza bowl on Saturdays.</u>

---

1. Monday it snowed.   Tuesday it snowed.   Wednesday it snowed.

_____

_____

2. Amber likes shopping.   Eliza like shopping.   I like shopping.

_____

_____

3. Derek was bored.   Derek was tired.   Derek was hungry.

_____

_____

4. The girl is sixteen.   The girl can drive a car.   The girl is named Eliza.

_____

_____

5. She went shopping.   She bought an attractive outfit.   The outfit was expensive.

_____

_____

Conjunctions and Dependent Clauses

Directions   Underline the dependent clause in each sentence. Rewrite each sentence on the line and add the correct punctuation.

> **EXAMPLE**   When Alice graduated from high school she received a diploma.
> <u>When Alice graduated from high school,</u> she received a diploma.

1. If Avery has a chance he will go to summer camp.

2. While he is there he will earn money as a counselor.

3. Although Avery will be busy he will find time for recreation.

4. He plans to swim every day after he finishes his chores.

5. Because he likes kids and the great outdoors Avery always enjoys camp.

Directions   Combine each pair of sentences using one of the subordinating conjunctions in the box. Write each new sentence on the line. Use the correct punctuation.

after	because	since
when	although	if
unless	while	

> **EXAMPLE**   Brian was out of town. Sarah celebrated her birthday.
> Brian was out of town <u>when</u> Sarah celebrated her birthday.

6. The storm was over. We went outside.

7. Dinner is ready. We can eat.

8. Camp is over. We will write letters to our new friends.

9. The tennis shoes are worn out. Cathy got new ones.

10. We plan to visit New Orleans. We are in Louisiana.

Writing a Paragraph

Directions Follow the steps listed below to write a paragraph. Indent the
first sentence of the paragraph.

Step 1 The beginning of the paragraph is called the **topic sentence**. It
states the main idea of a paragraph. Decide what subject you want
to write about. Write a topic sentence that tells the reader what the
paragraph is about.

Step 2 The middle of the paragraph is the **body**. The body tells about the
subject. It has examples, details, and explanations. Write three or
four sentences about the subject.

Step 3 The end of the paragraph is the **conclusion**. The last sentence of
the paragraph should summarize the main idea. Write the
conclusion to your paragraph.

Step 4 Write an interesting title for your paragraph.

Title: _____

_____

_____

_____

_____

_____

_____

_____

_____

_____

_____

_____

_____

_____

Identifying the Topic Sentence

Directions   Read each pair of topic sentences. Put a check mark (✓) on the line next to the better topic sentence in each pair.

1. A Ducks have many interesting characteristics.   _____

   B Ducks are animals that fly.   _____

2. A There is a wide variety of office furniture.   _____

   B When you furnish an office, select your
   desk and chair carefully.   _____

3. A An encyclopedia can be used a lot.   _____

   B An encyclopedia is a valuable book.   _____

4. A The police force has a variety of responsibilities.   _____

   B This paragraph will be about the police force.   _____

5. A Choosing a career is an important decision.   _____

   B There are many good careers available.   _____

6. A Fashion designs change frequently.   _____

   B Fashion designs change every season.   _____

7. A Swimming is one summer sport that I enjoy.   _____

   B Swimming is a sport.   _____

8. A The newspaper has information.   _____

   B The newspaper is an information source.   _____

9. A My favorite soap opera is "Hospital Life."   _____

   B There are many soap operas on TV.   _____

10. A There is a variety of animals at the zoo.   _____

   B I saw elephants, seals, polar bears, and monkeys at the zoo.   _____

Staying on the Topic

Directions Find the sentence in each paragraph that does not relate to the
paragraph topic. Underline the sentence.

1. It was a beautiful day for sailing. Juan decided to take his sailboat out on the lake.
   He sailed for an hour. Juan had homework to do. He passed several other sailboats
   while on the lake.

2. Exercise is important. It keeps your body healthy. Reading is an enjoyable hobby.
   Jogging and swimming are excellent forms of exercise. There are other effective
   forms of exercise.

3. The children wanted a pet. The children wanted new bicycles. Their mother said
   they could have a puppy or a kitten if they promised to take care of it. They
   promised they would care for it and then asked for a puppy.

4. Kim enjoys driving. She likes sports cars. Kim prefers sports cars with convertible
   tops. She also prefers sports cars that are either blue or green. If she ever gets a
   sports car, she wants one with a five-speed transmission.

5. David and Fran went to the zoo. They saw elephants and seals. They saw a polar
   bear swimming. David watched the ducks eat, and Fran saw the baby donkey get a
   bath. The zoo was crowded.

6. Cake decorating is a time-consuming job. The icing must be the right consistency.
   Then you must add a small amount of coloring to a small amount of icing. You
   must do this for each different color you use. Everyone will enjoy the cake. Then,
   using your colored icing, you decorate the cake with a picture or words.

7. Choosing a career is difficult, but not impossible. Try to choose a career that you
   are good at and will enjoy. Education is important. Salary may be a factor when
   choosing a career, but it may not be the deciding factor.

8. A train is a form of transportation. It travels by land. A train can take you places
   much faster than a car. An airplane travels by air.

9. Eggs are an important food. They provide a great deal of needed protein. Meat
   provides protein. Eggs can be eaten at any meal and cooked in a variety of ways.

10. Space exploration is very important to the United States. It allows the country to
    explore other planets. Space exploration also enables this country to set up space
    satellites for world communication. Mexico is not involved in space exploration.
    The United States has launched many space missions.

Identifying Strong Summaries and Conclusions

Directions Choose the better summary or conclusion for each paragraph.
Put a check mark next to it.

1. It is important to choose safe toys for children. Toys that are sharp or too small are not appropriate for babies or small children. Toys for older children should provide many hours of entertainment.

    A Books for children are also needed. _____

    B Well-chosen toys will only benefit your children. _____

2. Beginning swimmers are required to develop a variety of skills. Each skill encourages the swimmer to be comfortable in the water by building a swimmer's confidence.

    A Beginning swimmers are not expected to know every swimming stroke. _____

    B A swimmer's confidence will enable him or her to learn any swimming stroke. _____

3. There are many kinds of TV game shows. Though the shows are different, they all give away money, prizes, or both. The people who try to win are called contestants.

    A To win money, contestants answer questions or do certain tasks. _____

    B It is fun to win. _____

4. Presenting the right image at a job interview is extremely important. Your appearance and manner of speech will affect the interviewer's opinion. The way in which you answer the questions will also improve your chances of being hired.

    A Therefore, advance preparation is necessary for a successful interview. _____

    B When you get the job, you can do what you want. _____

5. The telephone can be an important tool in an emergency. If someone is sick, in trouble, or injured, a phone call can save a life.

    A You can use the telephone to call an ambulance or the police. _____

    B It is also helpful to use a phone to communicate with friends. _____

Giving Information and Explanations

Directions Read the paragraph. Then answer the questions, using complete sentences.

Life Insurance

Buying life insurance is important. You should be well informed about your choices. Insurance agents can explain the different kinds of insurance. They can tell you how to get the most insurance for your money. When you buy insurance, you will get a copy of the policy. Read the policy carefully to be sure you understand what you are buying. Keep the policy in a safe place in your home.

1. What is the main idea of the paragraph? State the main idea in another way.

_____

_____

_____

2. What are the reasons that the writer gives to explain that idea?

_____

_____

_____

3. What conclusion does the writer make? State the final sentence in another way.

_____

_____

_____

4. Is the main idea of the paragraph clear? How could this paragraph be improved?

_____

_____

_____

5. Write a different title for the paragraph.

_____

Writing a How-To Paragraph

Directions Read the following how-to paragraph. Then write sentences to answer the questions.

Shopping for an Automobile

Purchasing your first automobile is a big decision that requires careful planning. Your first step is deciding how much money you can spend. Count your cash and visit a bank to find out how much you can borrow. Now, with a price in mind, examine the automobiles in that price range. Make a list of your most important criteria. You may want a car with airbags. You may need a car with four doors. A car that has a warranty might be most important to you. Certainly, you want to take any car for a test drive. Most people ask an auto mechanic to check a car they are thinking about buying. All of these steps lead up to the day you make a decision and drive your car home.

1. What is the paragraph telling you how to do?

_____

_____

2. What is the first step in shopping for an automobile?

_____

_____

3. Find three transition words or phrases in the paragraph. Write them here.

_____

_____

_____

4. Write three things that the writer tells you to do before you purchase an automobile.

_____

_____

_____

5. Read the last sentence. Is this sentence a summary or a conclusion? Explain your answer.

_____

_____

Asking Questions to Gather Information

Directions   Imagine that you are shopping for each of the items listed below. Write three specific questions that you would ask the person who is offering each item. Write your questions as complete interrogative sentences.

EXAMPLE   You are buying a CD player.
A   What brands of CD players do you sell?
B   What is the price range of these CD players?
C   What kind of warranty is offered on the CD player I choose?

1. You are renting an apartment.

A _____

B _____

C _____

2. You are buying a new car.

A _____

B _____

C _____

3. You are selecting a new telephone.

A _____

B _____

C _____

4. You are adopting a puppy from an animal shelter.

A _____

B _____

C _____

5. You are ordering dinner in a restaurant.

A _____

B _____

C _____

Writing Persuasive Paragraphs

Directions   Read the following paragraph. Then answer the questions with sentences.

Dear Mom and Dad,

   As you know, I have a great need for reliable transportation. If I had my own car, I could drive myself to track practice. You would not need to pick me up every night. Also, I could help with family chores such as going to the grocery store. My reliability has been established without a doubt. My job at the gas station with Mrs. Lentz is going quite well. I think Mrs. Lentz will give me a good recommendation. Also, my job will provide the funds for gasoline and maintenance. My bank account is pretty solid since I have been saving most of my salary. Hopefully, these facts support my need for an automobile as well as proof of my dependability.

   Your deserving son,

   Derek

1. Whom is Derek trying to persuade in this paragraph?

   _____

2. What is he trying to persuade them to do?

   _____

   _____

3. How would Derek's having a car help his parents?

   _____

   _____

4. Who does Derek think will back him up in his mission? Why will she support him, and why is her opinion important?

   _____

   _____

   _____

5. What additional facts could you add to this paragraph to make it stronger?

   _____

   _____

   _____

Writing a Short Story

Directions Write a short story. Put the events in chronological order.
Write a title for your story. Then proofread your story.

Title: _____

_____

_____

_____

_____

_____

_____

_____

_____

_____

_____

_____

_____

_____

_____

_____

_____

_____

_____

Writing Strong Topic Sentences

Directions   Improve these topic sentences. Change words around.
Add more details.

1. You have to do things like practice and concentrate if you want to be good at baseball.

_____

_____

2. Novels that tell why people do things are good.

_____

_____

3. Old things that you can find in attics are interesting.

_____

_____

4. Different spices go into a lot of gourmet foods.

_____

_____

5. If one wants a good job, then one should have the skills to do it.

_____

_____

6. Swimmers ought to know rules that will help them to be safe.

_____

_____

7. If you want to enjoy something, look at a sunset.

_____

_____

8. Insects do things that human beings often do.

_____

_____

9. Even though Jill and Jean were twins, they were not the same.

_____

_____

10. There are a lot of things you can do with old newspapers.

_____

_____

Creating Interesting Sentences

Directions   Rewrite each sentence by changing the word order. Find a different word or phrase in the sentence to put at the beginning. Capitalize the first word and use end punctuation.

(EXAMPLES)   In the fall, the family usually goes camping.
      The family usually goes camping in the fall.
      Usually the family goes camping in the fall.

1. We seldom watch TV in the summer.

_____

2. We are usually too busy with outdoor activities.

_____

3. The weather is always sunny and warm where we live.

_____

4. We have not had much rain in our town lately.

_____

5. I heard thunder suddenly rumbling in the background.

_____

6. Everyone immediately was sure that we would have rain.

_____

7. The thunder stopped after a few minutes.

_____

8. We opened the door and looked outside slowly.

_____

9. The sky was clear as far as we could see at that moment.

_____

10. We will get some rain someday soon.

_____

Adding Transition Words and Phrases

Directions Rewrite these paragraphs to make them more interesting. Add some transition words or phrases such as *then, first, meanwhile, later, next, before, finally, also, at last,* or *in the meantime.*

1. Derek walked onto the tennis court. He was ready to serve. He tossed the ball into the air. He hit it hard. He really wanted to win the match.

_____

_____

_____

2. Amber watched the waves coming in. She looked around for her parents. She saw them. She decided to hold their hands. The ocean looked too rough today.

_____

_____

_____

3. Computers do many things to help us. They keep banking records. They solve difficult math problems. They even control traffic lights in big cities.

_____

_____

_____

4. Brandon studied the pitcher carefully. It was his turn to bat. A solid hit would bring in the winning run. He stepped up to the plate. His eyes followed the ball until it met his bat. He knew he helped win the game.

_____

_____

_____

5. Eliza wanted to make cookies for the bake sale. She turned on the oven. She gathered the ingredients she would need. She found a large mixing bowl and spoon. Eliza mixed the ingredients together. She spooned the cookie dough onto the cookie sheet and put it in the oven to bake.

_____

_____

_____

Direct and Indirect Comparisons

Directions Underline the comparisons in the following sentences. Decide whether the comparisons are direct (a metaphor) or indirect (a simile). Write *direct* or *indirect* on the line.

(EXAMPLES)   Judy is <u>a puzzle</u> to everyone.   ____direct____

The baby's skin is <u>as smooth as silk</u>.   ____indirect____

1. That song is like a beautiful dream.   _____

2. That skyscraper looks like the Empire State Building.   _____

3. My dog is as brave as Lassie.   _____

4. Aunt Edna is as old as the hills.   _____

5. Dan is a mountain of a man.   _____

6. A smile from Sally is as rare as an old coin.   _____

7. Our father is a rock of strength.   _____

8. Her skin is as smooth as velvet.   _____

9. Charlotte Church has the voice of an angel.   _____

10. Shirley has the agility of a deer.   _____

Directions Complete the statements below using direct or indirect comparisons. Be creative!

11. A cup of coffee in the morning is _____.

12. The sky grew as dark as _____.

13. Poetry is the _____.

14. The victory was like a _____.

15. Tomorrow will be as _____.

Writing a Short Answer to a Test Question

Directions Write a short answer for each question. Write your answers
in sentences. You may use a reference book.

1. What did Benjamin Franklin invent?

_____

_____

_____

2. Where is Yellowstone National Park?

_____

_____

_____

3. Who was Edgar Allan Poe?

_____

_____

_____

4. Where was the first permanent English
colonial settlement in America?

_____

_____

_____

5. Which planet is closest to the sun?

_____

_____

_____

6. What is the capital of the United States?

_____

_____

_____

7. Who was Christopher Columbus?

_____

_____

_____

8. What is the Pulitzer Prize awarded for?

_____

_____

_____

9. Who was the first president of the United
States?

_____

_____

_____

10. When did the Japanese bomb Pearl Harbor?

_____

_____

_____

Planning an Essay Answer

Directions Read the prompt carefully and answer the questions that
follow. Write your answers in sentences.

Prompt Twenty years ago, no one knew that everyone would be using computers in their daily lives.
No one knew that cell phones would be everyday technology. Imagine the next important
invention. Then write an essay about it. Use the back of this page if you need more
room to write.

1. What is the invention? Write one sentence identifying the invention and telling what it will do.

   _____

2. How will this invention change the way people do things? List a few ways.

   _____

   _____

3. What are some positive effects of this invention?

   _____

   _____

4. What are some negative effects of this invention?

   _____

   _____

5. Write a topic sentence that expresses the main idea for a paragraph about this invention.
Your sentence should express your point of view.

   _____

   _____

6. Now, organize your supporting ideas into several sentences that will be the body of your essay.

   _____

   _____

   _____

7. Write a one-sentence summary or conclusion for your essay.

   _____

8. Copy your essay onto another sheet of paper.

9. Write a title for your essay. _____

10. Check your grammar and spelling and correct any errors.

Writing an Essay Answer

Directions Read each group of items and the question that follows it.
Write an essay response to each question.

Facts About the Mammoth
- It no longer exists.
- It was a large elephant-like animal.
- It was about nine feet tall.
- It had long, curved tusks.
- Researchers believe it had hairy skin.

1. Describe the mammoth.

_____

_____

_____

_____

_____

Facts About Antarctica
- It is a continent.
- It is located around the South Pole.
- It is about 5,000,000 square miles in size.
- It is extremely cold there most of the year.
- Very little life exists there.

2. Describe Antarctica.

_____

_____

_____

_____

_____

_____

Facts About Mercury
- It is the closest planet to the sun.
- It has no moons.
- It takes 58 Earth days to rotate once on its axis.
- It takes the planet 88 Earth days to make one trip around the sun.
- It is only 36,000,000 miles from the sun.

3. Describe the planet Mercury.

_____

_____

_____

_____

_____

Facts About Global Warming
- It is an environmental problem caused by the greenhouse effect.
- Ecological disruption, floods, droughts, and disease are some consequences of it.
- Over time, average temperatures will be warmer and heat waves will be more frequent.
- Scientists predict that temperature changes could cause the polar ice caps to melt.

4. Describe global warming.

_____

_____

_____

_____

_____

Revising an Essay

Directions   Read the following paragraph. Find and circle these kinds of errors: spelling, capitalization, punctuation, and sentence fragments. Correct the errors and rewrite the improved paragraph on the lines.

Why I Quit Bowling

by Brandon Tucker

For many years, I enjoyed bowlling. Too year ago I quit my team and this be the reason why. The name of my team were the starframers. A starframe in bowling means that everyone gots a spare or a strike in that frame. We was great, everyones averages kept improving. Naturally, we was in first place all year. Finally it was the last nite of the season, my team had went into the final position round three games ahead of the second place teem. Confidence was our middle name that Night! We only had to win one game to take home the first place trophy. All I can says is that I is looking right now at a second place trophy. Yes, we lost all four games, surely, no more needs to be said.

_____

_____

_____

_____

_____

_____

_____

_____

_____

_____

_____

_____

_____

Writing a Message

When you take a message, be sure that it is complete. Remember, a message should include the following information:
- The time and date that you wrote the message
- The name of the person who gave you the information
- The information needed by the person who will receive the message
- Your name, to show who wrote the message

Directions Identify the information that is missing from each of the following messages. Write your answers on the lines.

EXAMPLE Dad, I'm going to the movies. I'll see you later.
<u>time, date, when he or she will be back, and who left the message</u>

---

1. Derek, we were supposed to go to the movies.
Sarah

_____

_____

2. Mom, my teacher called. She'll call back later.
Derek

_____

_____

3. Mr. Smith, I have a question about the assignment. I'll stop by later.

_____

_____

4. Eliza, Amber called. She wants you to go shopping. Call her back.

_____

_____

5. Sarah, Derek called.
Dad

_____

_____

Writing a Memo

Directions   Read the following two messages. Rewrite each one in memo
form. Use today's date.

September 10, 2003

Dear Mrs. Smith,
   Please excuse John Hall today at 1:00 P.M.
He has a doctor's appointment this afternoon
at 1:30 P.M.
                                   Mrs. K. Hall

May 5, 2004

Dear Mr. White,
   The student body would like to see more
school spirit and involvement. We would like
to plan a special Springfield High Sports Day.
Would you please help us in any way that
you can?
                                   Amber Choy

MEMO
Date: _____
To: _____
From: _____
Subject: _____
_____
_____
_____
_____
_____

MEMO
Date: _____
To: _____
From: _____
Subject: _____
_____
_____
_____
_____
_____

Understanding Electronic Mail (E-Mail) Messages

Directions   Use the sample e-mail message to answer the questions.

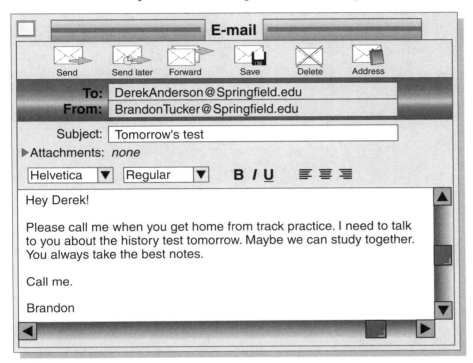

1. Who will receive this e-mail?

_____

2. Who sent it?

_____

3. What is Brandon's screen name?

_____

4. What is Brandon's complete e-mail address?

_____

5. What is the subject of this e-mail?

_____

6. What is the name of Derek's ISP?

_____

7. What type of provider is Springfield? How do you know?

_____

_____

8. What font did Brandon use?

_____

9. Are there any attachments to this e-mail?

_____

10. What does Brandon want Derek to do?

_____

Writing a Personal Letter

Directions Write a personal letter to a friend or a relative on the lines below. This letter may be an invitation, a thank-you, or just a letter to keep in touch. Remember to include the five parts of a personal letter: date, salutation (greeting), body, closing, and signature.

Writing a Business Letter

Directions Decide whether these greetings and closings are appropriate
for a business letter. Write *yes* or *no* on the line following
each one.

1. Dear Derek, _____

2. Cordially, _____

3. Gentlemen: _____

4. Your sister, _____

5. Dear Dr. Smith: _____

6. Your friend, _____

7. Yours truly, _____

8. Dear Aunt Betsy, _____

9. Sincerely, _____

10. Love, _____

Directions Name the eight parts of a business
letter. Circle the five parts that are
also included in personal letters.

11. _____

12. _____

13. _____

14. _____

15. _____

16. _____

17. _____

18. _____

Directions Name two ways in which a
business letter is different
from a personal letter.

19. _____

_____

_____

_____

20. _____

_____

_____

Writing Addresses

Directions Some sample addresses appear below. All of them are incorrect. Rewrite each one correctly.

Return Address ⟶

Christy Walker
3212 Harrigut Avenue, Apt. 201
Dayton, OH 45442

Mailing Address ⟶

Ms. Barbara Pearson
23 Tralee Way
San Rafael, CA 94903

1. Tony Pierce
Dartmouth Ct 17
Trenton, NJ 08601

1. _____
_____
_____

2. Janet Lahney
Apt. 13
College Park, MD 20740
92 Westland Drive

2. _____
_____
_____

3. Crystal Enterprises
Valerie Armstrong
67 Tulip Drive
19050 Lansdowne, PA

3. _____
_____
_____

4. Managing Editor
Fashion Trends
Sartoga avenue 4210
95129
CA San Jose

4. _____
_____
_____
_____

5. taffy clayton
Cumberland MD 21502
517 Louisville Lane

5. _____
_____
_____

Selecting a Topic

Directions Read each pair of topics. Decide which one is broad and which one is narrow. Write *broad* or *narrow* on the lines.

EXAMPLE **A** Cancer   __broad__
            B Treatment for cancer   __narrow__

---

1. A The first president, George Washington   _____

    B Presidents   _____

2. A Election process of Supreme Court judges   _____

    B Judges   _____

3. A Nutrition   _____

    B Vitamin deficiencies   _____

4. A Risks of smoking   _____

    B Smoking   _____

5. A United States history   _____

    B Europeans arrive in America   _____

6. A Computers   _____

    B Selecting a computer   _____

7. A Historical sites in Washington, D.C.   _____

    B Washington, D.C.   _____

8. A Education   _____

    B Funds from the federal government for education   _____

9. A Zebras   _____

    B Animals of Africa   _____

10. A Whole grains   _____

    B Brown rice   _____

Searching for Information

Directions Read each item. Decide whether you would look it up in a
library catalog by author, title, or subject. Write *author, title,* or
subject on each line.

(EXAMPLE) the climate of South America
<u>   subject   </u>

1. the population of Quebec

_____

2. the writings of Benjamin Franklin

_____

3. Nobel Prize winners in 1935

_____

4. *The World Almanac*

_____

5. Leap Year

_____

6. novels by Margaret Atwood

_____

7. *Treasure Island*

_____

8. the number of high school dropouts in 1980

_____

9. History of America

_____

10. *For Whom the Bell Tolls*

_____

Using Reference Materials

Directions Write the reference book you would use to find the answer to each question. Choose from *almanac, atlas, encyclopedia,* or *biographical dictionary.*

1. Which states border the Mississippi River? _____

2. Who is Nelson Mandela? _____

3. Who won the World Series in 2000? _____

4. What highways cross Texas? _____

5. Discuss the history of computers. _____

Directions Use the information in the catalog entry to answer the questions.

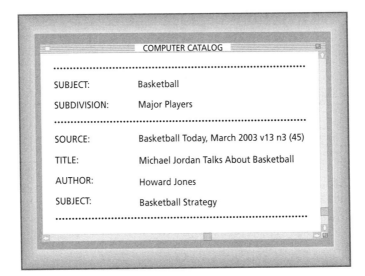

COMPUTER CATALOG

SUBJECT: Basketball

SUBDIVISION: Major Players

SOURCE: Basketball Today, March 2003 v13 n3 (45)

TITLE: Michael Jordan Talks About Basketball

AUTHOR: Howard Jones

SUBJECT: Basketball Strategy

6. Who is the author of this article? _____

7. What is this article probably about? _____

8. What is the title of the magazine? _____

9. In which volume does this article appear? _____

10. How long is this article? _____

Taking Notes

Directions   Read the paragraph. Take notes on the paragraph. Write your
notes on the lines.

      Wolfgang Amadeus Mozart is one of the world's most important
composers. He lived during the eighteenth century in Austria. He was born
in 1756 and died in 1791. Mozart composed some of the most famous
operas, including *The Magic Flute, The Marriage of Figaro,* and *Don
Giovanni.* Mozart was a child prodigy. At a very young age, he performed
on the piano all over Europe. A movie titled *Amadeus* about his life won
the Academy Award for best picture in 1984.

_____
_____
_____
_____
_____
_____
_____

Directions   Now paraphrase your notes in a paragraph of your own about
Mozart. Write your paraphrased notes on the lines.

_____
_____
_____
_____
_____
_____
_____

Creating an Outline

Directions Use Outline A as a guide. Rewrite Outline B in the correct
form on the back of this paper or on another sheet of paper.
Use correct punctuation. Indent the lines correctly. Capitalize
the first word of each topic and proper nouns.

EXAMPLE

Outline A
Nicaragua

I. Introduction
   A. Location
   B. Size
      1. Population
      2. Area

II. Geographical features
   A. Atlantic and Pacific coasts
   B. The Cordillera Mountains
   C. Volcanoes

III. Agriculture and industry
   A. Chief crops
      1. Bananas
      2. Cotton
   B. Minerals
      1. Gold
      2. Silver
      3. Copper

IV. Currency

V. Languages

VI. Summary and conclusions

Outline B
United Nations

Introduction
   a. location
   B. Buildings

II. General Assembly
   A. composed of
   b. sessions
   C. Budget and apportion expenses

3 Security Council
   A. Number of members
   b. purpose

4. Economic and Social Council
   A. Number of members
   b. purpose

V. Trusteeship Council

IV. Currency

VI Secretariat

VII International Court of Justice
   a Function
   B Election
      1. term
      2. Method

8 Summary and conclusion

Organizing Topics to Write a Report

Directions Follow the steps to organize the topics in a logical order.
Use outline form with correct punctuation.

Step 1 Identify the main topics.

Step 2 Identify the subtopics that belong with each main topic.

Step 3 Write the topics and subtopics in correct outline form
on the lines.

A Typical Home Office

Adding machine _____

Bookshelves _____

Tape _____

Chair _____

Computer _____

Desk _____

Modem _____

Office Furniture _____

Paper _____

Pens and pencils _____

Printer _____

Stapler _____

Supplies _____

Telephone _____

Types of Equipment _____

Work table _____

Creating a Bibliography

Directions Prepare a bibliography, using the facts about the five
publications listed below. Arrange the entries in alphabetical
order by the author's last name. If no author is listed, use the
first important word of the article or book title. Indent the
second line of each entry as well as any lines after that.

EXAMPLE   Pettis, A.M. <u>Basic Car Care.</u> New York: Simon & Schuster, 2003.

1. Jim Garner's book called <u>Using a Video Camera</u>. Published in 2001 in Chicago, IL, by Crown Books.

2. <u>You Can Be a Sports Announcer</u> by George Knott. Published in New York City by The New Publishers, Inc. in 2003.

3. "You Can Edit," by Christine Romero. Published in <u>Editor's Journal</u>, Volume 4, April 2003, pages 6–8.

4. <u>Editing for Fun and Profit</u> by Bob Oringel. Published in Bowie, MD, by the Bowie Community Television, October 2002.

5. "Video Editing" in the 2004 <u>Television Encyclopedia</u>, Vol. 11, pages 300–305.

BIBLIOGRAPHY

_____

_____

_____

_____

_____

_____

_____

_____

_____

_____

_____

_____